50 French Pastries for Home Bakers

By: Kelly Johnson

Table of Contents

- Croissants
- Pain au Chocolat
- Mille-Feuille
- Éclairs
- Choux Pastry
- Tarte Tatin
- Madeleines
- Canelés
- Opera Cake
- Paris-Brest
- Financiers
- Clafoutis
- Tarte aux Fraises (Strawberry Tart)
- Kouign-Amann
- Profiteroles
- Galette des Rois
- Baba au Rhum
- Flan Parisien
- Savarin
- Religieuse
- Tarte au Citron (Lemon Tart)
- Pain aux Raisins
- Gateau Basque
- Fraisier
- Saint-Honoré
- Beignets
- Chaussons aux Pommes (Apple Turnovers)
- Palmiers
- Pithivier
- Boules de Berlin
- Tarte Bourdaloue (Pear Almond Tart)
- Merveilleux
- Moelleux au Chocolat (Chocolate Lava Cake)
- Tuiles
- Crêpes Suzette

- Bûche de Noël
- Macarons
- Croquembouche
- Gâteau Opéra
- Pain d'épices (Spiced Bread)
- Biscuit Joconde
- Gâteau aux Noix (Walnut Cake)
- Bostock
- Dacquoise
- Nougat
- Roulade
- Florentines
- Quatre-Quarts (Pound Cake)
- Sablés
- Feuilletés

Classic Croissant

Ingredients:

Dough:

- 500g all-purpose flour
- 55g sugar
- 10g salt
- 10g instant yeast
- 300ml cold whole milk
- 30g unsalted butter (softened)

Butter Layer:

- 250g unsalted butter (cold)

Egg Wash:

- 1 egg
- 1 tbsp milk

Instructions:

1. **Prepare the Dough:** In a bowl, mix flour, sugar, salt, and yeast. Add cold milk and mix until a soft dough forms. Knead for 3-4 minutes. Add softened butter and knead for another 5 minutes until smooth. Shape the dough into a ball, wrap in plastic, and chill for 8 hours or overnight.
2. **Prepare the Butter Block:** Place the 250g cold butter between two sheets of parchment paper. Pound and roll it into a 20x20 cm (8x8 inch) square. Keep it chilled until ready to use.
3. **Incorporate the Butter:** Roll the dough into a 30x30 cm (12x12 inch) square. Place the butter block in the center at a 45-degree angle (like a diamond). Fold the dough's corners over the butter, sealing it completely.
4. **First Fold:** Roll the dough into a 60x20 cm (24x8 inch) rectangle. Fold into thirds (like folding a letter). This is your **first turn**. Wrap in plastic and chill for 30 minutes.
5. **Second and Third Turns:** Repeat the rolling and folding process two more times, chilling for 30 minutes between each turn.
6. **Shape the Croissants:** Roll the dough into a large 40x20 cm (16x8 inch) rectangle. Cut triangles about 8-10 cm wide at the base. Roll each triangle tightly

from the base to the tip to form the croissant shape. Place on a baking sheet lined with parchment paper.
7. **Proof:** Let the croissants rise in a warm place for 1-2 hours, until puffy.
8. **Egg Wash & Bake:** Preheat the oven to 200°C (390°F). Brush the croissants with egg wash. Bake for 15-20 minutes until golden brown.

Enjoy warm, flaky croissants straight from the oven!

Pain au Chocolat

Ingredients:

Dough:

- 500g all-purpose flour
- 55g sugar
- 10g salt
- 10g instant yeast
- 300ml cold whole milk
- 30g unsalted butter (softened)

Butter Layer:
- 250g unsalted butter (cold)

Filling:
- 100g dark chocolate bars or sticks

Egg Wash:
- 1 egg
- 1 tbsp milk

Instructions:

1. **Prepare the Dough:** In a bowl, mix flour, sugar, salt, and yeast. Add cold milk and mix until a soft dough forms. Knead for 3-4 minutes. Add softened butter and knead for another 5 minutes until smooth. Shape the dough into a ball, wrap in plastic, and chill for 8 hours or overnight. 2. **Prepare the Butter Block:** Place the cold butter between two sheets of parchment paper. Pound and roll it into a 20x20 cm (8x8 inch) square. Keep it chilled until ready to use. 3. **Incorporate the Butter:** Roll the dough into a 30x30 cm (12x12 inch) square. Place the butter block in the center at a 45-degree angle. Fold the dough's corners over the butter, sealing it completely. 4. **First Fold:** Roll the dough into a 60x20 cm (24x8 inch) rectangle. Fold into thirds. Wrap in plastic and chill for 30 minutes. 5. **Second and Third Turns:** Repeat the rolling and folding process twice more, chilling for 30 minutes between turns. 6. **Shape the Pain au Chocolat:** Roll the dough into a large 40x20 cm (16x8 inch) rectangle. Cut into rectangles about 8x10 cm (3x4 inches). Place a chocolate stick at each end and roll tightly from both sides towards the center. 7. **Proof:** Let the pastries rise for 1-2 hours until puffy. 8. **Egg Wash & Bake:** Preheat the oven to 200°C (390°F). Brush with egg wash and bake for 15-20 minutes until golden brown.

Mille-Feuille

Ingredients:

Puff Pastry:

- 500g store-bought or homemade puff pastry
  Pastry Cream:
- 500ml whole milk
- 4 egg yolks
- 100g sugar
- 40g cornstarch
- 1 vanilla bean or 1 tsp vanilla extract
- 50g unsalted butter
  Icing:
- 150g powdered sugar
- 2-3 tbsp milk
- 50g dark chocolate

Instructions:

1. **Prepare the Pastry Cream:** Heat the milk and vanilla in a saucepan until simmering. Whisk egg yolks, sugar, and cornstarch in a bowl. Gradually pour the hot milk over the mixture, whisking constantly. Return to the saucepan and cook until thickened. Remove from heat, add butter, and chill. 2. **Bake the Puff Pastry:** Preheat the oven to 200°C (390°F). Roll the puff pastry into thin sheets. Bake on a parchment-lined sheet with another tray on top to prevent rising. Bake for 20-25 minutes until golden. 3. **Assemble the Mille-Feuille:** Cut the pastry into equal rectangles. Spread pastry cream between layers, stacking 3 sheets high. 4. **Icing:** Mix powdered sugar and milk to make a glaze. Drizzle melted chocolate over the top in lines, then drag a toothpick across to create the signature pattern. 5. **Chill and Serve:** Let the mille-feuille set in the fridge for 1-2 hours before serving.

Éclairs

Ingredients:

Choux Pastry:

- 125ml water
- 125ml whole milk
- 100g unsalted butter
- 1/2 tsp salt
- 150g all-purpose flour
- 4 large eggs

Pastry Cream:
- 500ml whole milk
- 4 egg yolks
- 100g sugar
- 40g cornstarch
- 50g unsalted butter

Chocolate Glaze:
- 200g dark chocolate
- 100ml heavy cream

Instructions:

1. **Prepare the Choux Pastry:** Preheat the oven to 190°C (375°F). Heat water, milk, butter, and salt in a saucepan. Once boiling, add flour and stir vigorously until a dough forms. Cook for 1-2 minutes to remove moisture. Cool slightly, then beat in eggs one at a time until smooth. 2. **Pipe the Éclairs:** Transfer the dough to a piping bag with a round tip. Pipe 10-12 cm (4-5 inch) logs onto a baking sheet. Bake for 25-30 minutes until golden. Cool completely. 3. **Prepare the Pastry Cream:** Heat the milk in a saucepan. Whisk egg yolks, sugar, and cornstarch in a bowl. Gradually whisk in the hot milk and return to the saucepan. Cook until thickened, remove from heat, add butter, and chill. 4. **Fill the Éclairs:** Cut a slit in each éclair or use a piping bag to fill them with pastry cream. 5. **Chocolate Glaze:** Melt dark chocolate and heavy cream together. Dip the top of each éclair in the glaze. 6. **Chill and Serve:** Let the glaze set before serving. Enjoy these classic French pastries!

Choux Pastry

Ingredients:

- 125ml water
- 125ml whole milk
- 100g unsalted butter
- 1/2 tsp salt
- 150g all-purpose flour
- 4 large eggs

Instructions:

1. Preheat the oven to 190°C (375°F). Heat water, milk, butter, and salt in a saucepan. Once boiling, add flour and stir vigorously until the dough forms a ball. 2. Cook for 1-2 minutes to remove moisture, then cool slightly. 3. Beat in the eggs one at a time until the dough becomes smooth and glossy. 4. Transfer to a piping bag and pipe onto a baking sheet. 5. Bake for 25-30 minutes until golden brown.

Tarte Tatin

Ingredients:

- 1 sheet puff pastry
- 6-8 apples (peeled and quartered)
- 100g sugar
- 50g unsalted butter

Instructions:

1. Preheat the oven to 190°C (375°F). In a pan, melt the sugar and butter to make a caramel. 2. Add apples and cook for 10 minutes until softened. 3. Place the apples in a baking dish and cover with puff pastry, tucking in the edges. 4. Bake for 30-35 minutes until the pastry is golden. 5. Invert onto a plate to serve.

Madeleines

Ingredients:

- 120g flour
- 100g sugar
- 2 large eggs
- 100g melted butter
- 1 tsp baking powder
- Zest of 1 lemon

Instructions:

1. Preheat the oven to 180°C (350°F). Beat eggs and sugar until pale and fluffy. 2. Fold in flour, baking powder, lemon zest, and melted butter. 3. Spoon the batter into greased madeleine molds. 4. Bake for 10-12 minutes until golden.

Canelés

Ingredients:

- 500ml whole milk
- 50g butter
- 100g flour
- 200g sugar
- 2 eggs + 2 yolks
- 1 tsp vanilla extract
- 2 tbsp dark rum

Instructions:

1. Heat the milk and butter until melted. 2. In a bowl, whisk eggs, yolks, sugar, and flour. Slowly add the milk mixture and stir in vanilla and rum. 3. Chill the batter for 24 hours. 4. Preheat the oven to 200°C (390°F). Pour the batter into greased canelé molds and bake for 50-60 minutes.

Opera Cake

Ingredients:

Sponge Cake:

- 4 eggs
- 100g sugar
- 100g almond flour
- 50g all-purpose flour
- 50g melted butter

Filling & Glaze:

- 200ml coffee syrup
- 200g dark chocolate ganache
- 200g coffee buttercream

Instructions:

1. Preheat the oven to 180°C (350°F). Beat eggs and sugar until fluffy, then fold in almond flour, all-purpose flour, and melted butter. 2. Bake the sponge cake in thin layers. 3. Assemble by layering cake with coffee syrup, ganache, and buttercream. 4. Finish with a chocolate glaze and chill.

Paris-Brest

Ingredients:

- 1 batch choux pastry
- 200ml heavy cream
- 2 tbsp sugar
- 100g praline paste

Instructions:

1. Pipe the choux pastry into a ring and bake at 190°C (375°F) for 25-30 minutes. 2. Whip the heavy cream with sugar until soft peaks form. 3. Fold in the praline paste. 4. Slice the pastry in half, fill with praline cream, and serve.

Financiers

Ingredients:

- 120g butter
- 100g almond flour
- 120g powdered sugar
- 40g flour
- 4 egg whites

Instructions:

1. Preheat the oven to 180°C (350°F). Brown the butter and let it cool. 2. Mix almond flour, powdered sugar, and flour. 3. Stir in the egg whites and browned butter. 4. Pour into molds and bake for 12-15 minutes.

Clafoutis

Ingredients:

- 500g cherries
- 100g flour
- 100g sugar
- 3 eggs
- 300ml milk
- 1 tsp vanilla extract

Instructions:

1. Preheat the oven to 180°C (350°F). Butter a baking dish and arrange the cherries in it. 2. Whisk the eggs, sugar, flour, milk, and vanilla together. 3. Pour the batter over the cherries. 4. Bake for 35-40 minutes until set and golden. Enjoy these delicious French desserts!

Tarte aux Fraises (Strawberry Tart)

Ingredients:

Pâte Sablée:

- 250g all-purpose flour
- 125g unsalted butter (cold and cubed)
- 80g powdered sugar
- 1 egg yolk
- 1-2 tbsp cold water
  Filling:
- 500g fresh strawberries (sliced)
- 250g pastry cream
- 2 tbsp apricot jam (for glazing)

Instructions:

1. **Make the Pâte Sablée:** In a bowl, combine flour and powdered sugar. Add cold butter and mix until crumbly. Add egg yolk and enough cold water to form a dough. Chill for 30 minutes. 2. Preheat the oven to 180°C (350°F). Roll out the dough and fit it into a tart pan. Prick the base with a fork and bake for 15-20 minutes until golden. 3. **Prepare the Filling:** Spread pastry cream over the cooled tart shell. Arrange sliced strawberries on top. 4. **Glaze:** Heat apricot jam until melted, then brush over the strawberries. Chill before serving.

Kouign-Amann

Ingredients:

- 500g all-purpose flour
- 250ml water
- 10g salt
- 10g instant yeast
- 300g unsalted butter (cold)
- 200g sugar

Instructions:

1. **Prepare the Dough:** In a bowl, mix flour, salt, and yeast. Add water and knead until smooth. Let rise for 1 hour. 2. **Butter Block:** Roll cold butter into a rectangle. 3. **Incorporate Butter:** Roll the dough into a rectangle, place the butter block in the center, and fold the dough over. Roll and fold the dough several times, chilling between folds. 4. **Shape:** Roll into a rectangle, sprinkle with sugar, fold, and cut into squares. 5. **Bake:** Preheat the oven to 200°C (390°F). Place squares in a pan and bake for 25-30 minutes until golden.

Profiteroles

Ingredients:

- 125ml water
- 125ml whole milk
- 100g unsalted butter
- 1/2 tsp salt
- 150g all-purpose flour
- 4 large eggs
- 200ml whipped cream
- Chocolate sauce (for serving)

Instructions:

1. **Prepare the Choux Pastry:** Preheat the oven to 190°C (375°F). Heat water, milk, butter, and salt in a saucepan. Once boiling, add flour and stir vigorously until a dough forms. 2. Cook for 1-2 minutes, cool slightly, then add eggs one at a time until smooth. 3. Pipe small balls onto a baking sheet and bake for 25-30 minutes until golden. 4. **Fill:** Cool and cut in half, filling with whipped cream. Drizzle with chocolate sauce before serving.

Galette des Rois

Ingredients:

Puff Pastry:

- 2 sheets store-bought puff pastry
  Frangipane Filling:
- 100g almond flour
- 100g sugar
- 100g unsalted butter (softened)
- 2 eggs
- 1 tsp vanilla extract

Instructions:

1. **Prepare the Frangipane Filling:** In a bowl, beat butter and sugar until creamy. Add almond flour, eggs, and vanilla, mixing until smooth. 2. Preheat the oven to 200°C (390°F). Roll out one sheet of puff pastry on a baking tray. 3. Spread the frangipane filling in the center, leaving a border. 4. Cover with the second pastry sheet, sealing the edges. Make a small hole in the top for steam. 5. Bake for 30-35 minutes until golden brown.

Baba au Rhum

Ingredients:

- 250g all-purpose flour
- 20g sugar
- 5g salt
- 10g instant yeast
- 3 large eggs
- 100ml milk
- 100g unsalted butter (melted)
- **Rum Syrup:**
- 200ml water
- 200g sugar
- 100ml dark rum

Instructions:

1. **Prepare the Dough:** In a bowl, mix flour, sugar, salt, and yeast. Add eggs, milk, and melted butter, and knead until smooth. Let rise for 1 hour. 2. Preheat the oven to 180°C (350°F). Grease baba molds and fill with dough. Bake for 20-25 minutes until golden. 3. **Prepare the Syrup:** Boil water and sugar until dissolved, then add rum. 4. Soak the cooled babas in the syrup before serving.

Flan Parisien

Ingredients:

- 1 sheet puff pastry
- 500ml milk
- 100g sugar
- 4 large eggs
- 40g cornstarch
- 1 tsp vanilla extract

Instructions:

1. Preheat the oven to 180°C (350°F). Roll out the puff pastry and line a tart pan. 2. In a saucepan, heat milk and sugar. In a bowl, whisk eggs, cornstarch, and vanilla. Gradually add hot milk to the egg mixture, then return to the pan. Cook until thickened. 3. Pour the mixture into the pastry shell and bake for 30-35 minutes until set and lightly browned.

Savarin

Ingredients:

- 250g all-purpose flour
- 20g sugar
- 5g salt
- 10g instant yeast
- 3 large eggs
- 100ml milk
- 100g unsalted butter (melted)
  Rum Syrup:
- 200ml water
- 200g sugar
- 100ml dark rum

Instructions:

1. **Prepare the Dough:** In a bowl, mix flour, sugar, salt, and yeast. Add eggs, milk, and melted butter, and knead until smooth. Let rise for 1 hour. 2. Preheat the oven to 180°C (350°F). Grease a savarin mold and fill with dough. Bake for 20-25 minutes until golden. 3. **Prepare the Syrup:** Boil water and sugar until dissolved, then add rum. 4. Soak the cooled savarin in the syrup before serving.

Religieuse

Ingredients:

Choux Pastry:

- 125ml water
- 125ml whole milk
- 100g unsalted butter
- 1/2 tsp salt
- 150g all-purpose flour
- 4 large eggs

Pastry Cream:
- 500ml whole milk
- 4 egg yolks
- 100g sugar
- 40g cornstarch

Chocolate Glaze:
- 200g dark chocolate
- 100ml heavy cream

Instructions:

1. **Prepare the Choux Pastry:** Preheat the oven to 190°C (375°F). Heat water, milk, butter, and salt in a saucepan. Once boiling, add flour and stir until a dough forms. 2. Cook for 1-2 minutes, cool slightly, then add eggs one at a time until smooth. 3. Pipe small balls for the base and larger ones for the top onto a baking sheet and bake for 25-30 minutes until golden. 4. **Prepare the Pastry Cream:** Heat the milk in a saucepan. Whisk egg yolks, sugar, and cornstarch in a bowl. Gradually whisk in the hot milk and return to the saucepan. Cook until thickened, remove from heat. 5. **Fill the Éclairs:** Cut a slit in each and fill with pastry cream. 6. **Chocolate Glaze:** Melt dark chocolate and heavy cream together. Dip the top of each religieuse in the glaze and stack. Enjoy these delightful French pastries!

Tarte au Citron (Lemon Tart)

Ingredients:

Pâte Sablée:

- 250g all-purpose flour
- 125g unsalted butter (cold and cubed)
- 80g powdered sugar
- 1 egg yolk
- 1-2 tbsp cold water

Lemon Filling:

- 4 large eggs
- 150g granulated sugar
- 100ml fresh lemon juice
- Zest of 2 lemons
- 100g unsalted butter (melted)

Instructions:

1. **Make the Pâte Sablée:** In a bowl, combine flour and powdered sugar. Add cold butter and mix until crumbly. Add egg yolk and enough cold water to form a dough. Chill for 30 minutes. 2. Preheat the oven to 180°C (350°F). Roll out the dough and fit it into a tart pan. Prick the base with a fork and bake for 15-20 minutes until golden. 3. **Prepare the Lemon Filling:** In a bowl, whisk together eggs, sugar, lemon juice, and zest until combined. Gradually stir in melted butter. 4. Pour the filling into the baked tart shell and bake for another 20-25 minutes until set. Cool before serving.

Pain aux Raisins

Ingredients:

- 500g puff pastry
- 100g pastry cream
- 150g raisins
- 50g sugar
- 1 egg (for egg wash)

Instructions:

1. **Prepare the Pastry Cream:** Make a basic pastry cream and let it cool. 2. Preheat the oven to 200°C (390°F). Roll out the puff pastry into a rectangle. 3. Spread the cooled pastry cream evenly over the pastry, then sprinkle with raisins and sugar. 4. Roll the pastry tightly and slice into rounds. Place on a baking sheet and brush with egg wash. 5. Bake for 20-25 minutes until golden brown and puffed.

Gâteau Basque

Ingredients:

Dough:

- 250g all-purpose flour
- 125g unsalted butter (softened)
- 100g sugar
- 1 egg
- 1 tsp vanilla extract
- 1 tsp baking powder

Filling:
- 200g pastry cream or cherry jam

Instructions:

1. **Make the Dough:** In a bowl, cream together butter and sugar until light and fluffy. Add egg, vanilla, and mix well. Gradually incorporate flour and baking powder until a smooth dough forms. 2. Divide the dough into two portions. Press one portion into the bottom of a tart pan. 3. Spread the filling evenly over the dough. Cover with the second portion of dough, sealing the edges. 4. Preheat the oven to 180°C (350°F) and bake for 30-35 minutes until golden.

Fraisier

Ingredients:

Sponge Cake:

- 4 large eggs
- 120g granulated sugar
- 120g all-purpose flour
- 1/2 tsp baking powder
  Strawberry Filling:
- 500g fresh strawberries (hulled and sliced)
- 200ml heavy cream (whipped)
- 100g pastry cream

Instructions:

1. **Prepare the Sponge Cake:** Preheat the oven to 180°C (350°F). In a bowl, whisk eggs and sugar until pale and thick. Fold in flour and baking powder gently. 2. Pour into a lined baking tray and bake for 10-15 minutes until golden. Let cool. 3. **Assemble the Cake:** Cut the sponge cake in half. Place one layer in a mold, fill with whipped cream and strawberries, then top with the second layer. 4. Chill for a few hours, then remove from the mold and serve.

Saint-Honoré

Ingredients:

- 250g puff pastry
- 125ml water
- 125ml whole milk
- 100g unsalted butter
- 1/2 tsp salt
- 150g all-purpose flour
- 4 large eggs

Chantilly Cream:

- 250ml heavy cream (whipped)
- 50g powdered sugar

Instructions:

1. **Prepare the Choux Pastry:** Preheat the oven to 190°C (375°F). Heat water, milk, butter, and salt in a saucepan until boiling. Add flour and stir until a dough forms. Cook for 1-2 minutes, then cool slightly. 2. Add eggs one at a time, mixing until smooth. Pipe small balls onto a baking sheet and bake for 25-30 minutes until golden. 3. **Assemble:** Bake the puff pastry into a round base. Fill with Chantilly cream and decorate with baked choux filled with cream.

Beignets

Ingredients:

- 250g all-purpose flour
- 50g sugar
- 1 tsp instant yeast
- 1/2 tsp salt
- 2 large eggs
- 100ml milk (warm)
- Oil (for frying)

Instructions:

1. **Prepare the Dough:** In a bowl, combine flour, sugar, yeast, and salt. Add eggs and warm milk, mixing until a dough forms. Knead until smooth, then let rise for 1 hour. 2. Heat oil in a deep pan. Roll out the dough and cut into squares. Fry until golden brown on both sides. 3. Drain on paper towels and sprinkle with powdered sugar before serving.

Chaussons aux Pommes (Apple Turnovers)

Ingredients:

- 500g puff pastry
- 3 apples (peeled and diced)
- 100g sugar
- 1 tsp cinnamon
- 1 egg (for egg wash)

Instructions:

1. **Prepare the Filling:** In a saucepan, cook diced apples with sugar and cinnamon until tender. Let cool. 2. Preheat the oven to 200°C (390°F). Roll out the puff pastry and cut into squares. 3. Place a spoonful of apple filling in the center of each square. Fold over and seal the edges. 4. Brush with egg wash and bake for 20-25 minutes until golden brown.

Palmiers

Ingredients:

- 250g puff pastry
- 100g granulated sugar
- 1 tsp vanilla extract

Instructions:

1. **Prepare the Dough:** Roll out the puff pastry into a rectangle. Sprinkle sugar evenly over the surface. 2. Roll each side of the rectangle towards the center, then chill for 30 minutes. 3. Preheat the oven to 200°C (390°F). Slice the rolled pastry into 1cm thick pieces. 4. Bake for 15-20 minutes until caramelized and golden. Enjoy these crisp and sweet pastries!

Pithivier

Ingredients:

- 500g puff pastry
- 200g almond cream
- 1 egg (for egg wash)
- 50g powdered sugar

Instructions:

1. Preheat the oven to 200°C (390°F). Roll out half of the puff pastry and cut into a circle for the base. 2. Spread the almond cream in the center, leaving a border. Roll out the second half of the pastry and place on top. Seal the edges and make a decorative pattern on top. 3. Brush with egg wash and bake for 25-30 minutes until golden brown. Dust with powdered sugar before serving.

Boules de Berlin

Ingredients:

- 500g all-purpose flour
- 100g sugar
- 20g fresh yeast
- 250ml milk (warm)
- 100g unsalted butter (melted)
- 3 large eggs
- Oil (for frying)
- Jam (for filling)

Instructions:

1. In a bowl, dissolve yeast in warm milk. Add flour, sugar, eggs, and melted butter, mixing until a dough forms. Knead until smooth and let rise for 1-2 hours. 2. Heat oil in a deep pan. Shape dough into balls and fry until golden brown. 3. Let cool and fill with jam using a piping bag. Dust with powdered sugar before serving.

Tarte Bourdaloue (Pear Almond Tart)

Ingredients:

Pâte Sablée:

- 250g all-purpose flour
- 125g unsalted butter (cold and cubed)
- 80g powdered sugar
- 1 egg yolk
- 1-2 tbsp cold water
  Almond Cream:
- 100g butter (softened)
- 100g sugar
- 100g ground almonds
- 2 large eggs
- 2 ripe pears (peeled and sliced)

Instructions:

1. **Prepare the Pâte Sablée:** In a bowl, combine flour, powdered sugar, and butter. Mix until crumbly. Add egg yolk and cold water to form a dough. Chill for 30 minutes. 2. Preheat the oven to 180°C (350°F). Roll out the dough and fit it into a tart pan. Bake for 15 minutes. 3. **Make the Almond Cream:** Beat together butter, sugar, ground almonds, and eggs until smooth. Pour the almond cream into the tart shell. 4. Arrange pear slices on top and bake for another 30 minutes until set.

Merveilleux

Ingredients:

- 4 large egg whites
- 250g granulated sugar
- 200g heavy cream (whipped)
- 100g chocolate shavings

Instructions:

1. **Prepare the Meringue:** Preheat the oven to 100°C (210°F). Whip egg whites until soft peaks form. Gradually add sugar and continue whipping until stiff peaks form. 2. Pipe meringue into small rounds on a baking sheet and bake for 1-2 hours until dry. Let cool. 3. **Assemble:** Sandwich two meringues with whipped cream and coat the outside with cream and chocolate shavings.

Moelleux au Chocolat (Chocolate Lava Cake)

Ingredients:

- 200g dark chocolate
- 100g unsalted butter
- 100g sugar
- 4 large eggs
- 50g all-purpose flour

Instructions:

1. Preheat the oven to 200°C (390°F). Melt chocolate and butter together in a bowl over simmering water. 2. In another bowl, whisk eggs and sugar until thick and pale. 3. Gradually add melted chocolate to the egg mixture, then fold in flour until combined. 4. Grease ramekins and fill with batter. Bake for 10-12 minutes until the edges are set but the center is soft. Let cool for a minute before inverting onto plates.

Tuiles

Ingredients:

- 100g all-purpose flour
- 100g powdered sugar
- 100g unsalted butter (melted)
- 2 large egg whites
- Almond slices (for decoration)

Instructions:

1. Preheat the oven to 180°C (350°F). In a bowl, mix flour, powdered sugar, melted butter, and egg whites until smooth. 2. Drop spoonfuls of the batter onto a baking sheet lined with parchment paper, flattening into thin rounds. 3. Sprinkle with almond slices. Bake for 5-7 minutes until golden. Let cool on a wire rack before serving.

Crêpes Suzette

Ingredients:

Crêpes:

- 250g all-purpose flour
- 3 large eggs
- 500ml milk
- 50g unsalted butter (melted)

Sauce:
- 100g sugar
- 100ml orange juice
- Zest of 1 orange
- 50ml Grand Marnier or orange liqueur

Instructions:

1. **Make the Crêpes:** In a bowl, whisk flour, eggs, and milk until smooth. Stir in melted butter. Heat a non-stick pan and pour in batter, cooking each crêpe for 1-2 minutes on each side. 2. **Prepare the Sauce:** In a saucepan, combine sugar, orange juice, and zest. Cook until syrupy, then add the liqueur. 3. Fold crêpes into quarters and place in the sauce, allowing them to soak for a minute before serving.

Bûche de Noël

Ingredients:

Sponge Cake:

- 4 large eggs
- 100g granulated sugar
- 100g all-purpose flour
- 30g cocoa powder

Filling:

- 200g heavy cream (whipped)
- 50g powdered sugar
- 100g dark chocolate (for ganache)
- 50ml heavy cream (for ganache)

Instructions:

1. **Make the Sponge Cake:** Preheat the oven to 180°C (350°F). Beat eggs and sugar until thick. Fold in flour and cocoa powder gently. Bake in a lined baking tray for 10-12 minutes. 2. Roll the cake in a towel to cool. 3. **Prepare the Filling:** Whip cream with powdered sugar. Unroll the cooled cake, spread the whipped cream, and re-roll it. 4. **Make the Ganache:** Heat cream and pour over chopped chocolate. Stir until smooth. Coat the log with ganache and decorate as desired before serving.

Macarons

Ingredients:

- 200g almond flour
- 200g powdered sugar
- 150g egg whites (aged)
- 50g granulated sugar
- Food coloring (optional)
- Filling of choice (buttercream, ganache, or jam)

Instructions:

1. Preheat the oven to 150°C (300°F). In a bowl, mix almond flour and powdered sugar. Sift to remove lumps. 2. Whip egg whites until frothy, then gradually add granulated sugar, whipping until stiff peaks form. Add food coloring if desired. 3. Gently fold in the almond mixture until combined. Pipe small circles onto a baking sheet lined with parchment paper. 4. Let sit for 30-60 minutes until a skin forms. Bake for 12-15 minutes. Cool before filling with the chosen filling.

Croquembouche

Ingredients:

Choux Pastry:

- 250ml water
- 100g unsalted butter
- 150g all-purpose flour
- 4 large eggs
  Caramel:
- 200g granulated sugar
- 50ml water

Instructions:

1. Preheat the oven to 200°C (390°F). In a saucepan, bring water and butter to a boil. Stir in flour until a dough forms. Remove from heat and let cool slightly. 2. Beat in eggs one at a time until smooth. Pipe small mounds onto a baking sheet and bake for 25-30 minutes until golden. 3. **Make the Caramel:** In a saucepan, dissolve sugar in water over medium heat. Allow to caramelize. 4. Assemble by dipping the tops of choux pastries in caramel and stacking them into a cone shape.

Gâteau Opéra

Ingredients:

Sponge Cake:

- 100g almond flour
- 100g powdered sugar
- 100g all-purpose flour
- 4 large eggs
- 50g butter (melted)

Coffee Buttercream:
- 200g unsalted butter (softened)
- 200g powdered sugar
- 2 tbsp strong coffee

Chocolate Ganache:
- 200g dark chocolate
- 200ml heavy cream

Instructions:

1. Preheat the oven to 180°C (350°F). In a bowl, combine almond flour, powdered sugar, and flour. Add eggs and melted butter, mixing until smooth. Bake in a rectangular pan for 15-20 minutes. 2. **Prepare the Ganache:** Heat cream and pour over chopped chocolate, stirring until smooth. 3. **Make the Buttercream:** Beat butter and powdered sugar until fluffy. Add coffee and mix. 4. Layer the sponge with buttercream and ganache, refrigerating between layers. Cut into rectangles to serve.

Pain d'épices (Spiced Bread)

Ingredients:

- 250g honey
- 200ml milk
- 250g all-purpose flour
- 100g dark brown sugar
- 1 tsp baking powder
- 1 tsp ground cinnamon
- 1/2 tsp ground ginger
- 1/4 tsp ground cloves
- 1/4 tsp ground nutmeg
- 2 large eggs

Instructions:

1. Preheat the oven to 160°C (320°F). In a saucepan, heat honey and milk until warm. 2. In a bowl, mix flour, sugar, baking powder, and spices. Add honey mixture and eggs, stirring until combined. 3. Pour into a greased loaf pan and bake for 40-50 minutes until a toothpick comes out clean. Let cool before slicing.

Biscuit Joconde

Ingredients:

- 250g almond flour
- 250g powdered sugar
- 6 large eggs
- 150g all-purpose flour
- 30g unsalted butter (melted)

Instructions:

1. Preheat the oven to 200°C (390°F). In a bowl, beat almond flour, powdered sugar, and eggs until thick and pale. 2. Gently fold in flour and melted butter. Spread the batter evenly onto a baking sheet lined with parchment paper. 3. Bake for 10-12 minutes until golden. Let cool before using in layered desserts.

Gâteau aux Noix (Walnut Cake)

Ingredients:

- 200g walnuts (ground)
- 150g all-purpose flour
- 200g granulated sugar
- 4 large eggs
- 100g unsalted butter (melted)
- 1 tsp baking powder

Instructions:

1. Preheat the oven to 180°C (350°F). In a bowl, beat eggs and sugar until fluffy. 2. Add ground walnuts, flour, and baking powder, mixing until combined. 3. Stir in melted butter and pour into a greased cake pan. Bake for 30-35 minutes until golden and a toothpick comes out clean. Let cool before serving.

Bostock

Ingredients:

- 4 slices of stale brioche
- 100g almond cream
- 100ml milk
- 50g sugar
- 2 large eggs
- Almond slices (for topping)

Instructions:

1. Preheat the oven to 180°C (350°F). In a bowl, whisk together milk, sugar, and eggs. Dip brioche slices in the mixture and place on a baking sheet. 2. Spread almond cream on top of each slice and sprinkle with almond slices. 3. Bake for 15-20 minutes until golden.

Dacquoise

Ingredients:

- 200g almond flour
- 200g powdered sugar
- 6 large egg whites
- 100g granulated sugar

Instructions:

1. Preheat the oven to 160°C (320°F). Whip egg whites until soft peaks form. Gradually add granulated sugar, continuing to whip until stiff peaks form. 2. Fold in almond flour and powdered sugar gently. 3. Pipe into rounds on a baking sheet and bake for 25-30 minutes until firm. Let cool before using in layered desserts.

Nougat

Ingredients:

- 200g honey
- 200g granulated sugar
- 100ml water
- 3 large egg whites
- 200g mixed nuts (almonds, pistachios, hazelnuts)
- 100g dried fruits (optional)

Instructions:

1. In a saucepan, combine honey, sugar, and water. Bring to a boil and cook until it reaches 145°C (293°F) on a sugar thermometer.
2. In a separate bowl, whip egg whites until stiff peaks form. Gradually pour the hot sugar mixture into the egg whites while continuing to whip.
3. Once combined, fold in mixed nuts and dried fruits if using. Spread into a greased mold and let cool completely before cutting into squares.

Roulade

Ingredients:

- 4 large eggs
- 100g granulated sugar
- 100g all-purpose flour
- 1 tsp vanilla extract
- Whipped cream or filling of choice

Instructions:

1. Preheat the oven to 180°C (350°F). Beat eggs and sugar until thick and pale. Fold in flour and vanilla extract gently.
2. Pour the batter onto a lined baking sheet, spreading it evenly. Bake for 10-12 minutes until golden.
3. Turn the cake onto a clean kitchen towel sprinkled with sugar. Remove the parchment paper and roll the cake tightly in the towel. Let cool completely.
4. Unroll the cake, spread with whipped cream or desired filling, and re-roll. Dust with powdered sugar before serving.

Florentines

Ingredients:

- 200g mixed nuts (almonds, hazelnuts)
- 100g candied fruit (orange, cherries)
- 100g sugar
- 100g heavy cream
- 200g dark chocolate (for dipping)

Instructions:

1. Preheat the oven to 180°C (350°F). Chop nuts and candied fruit finely.
2. In a saucepan, combine sugar and cream, cooking over medium heat until boiling. Stir in nuts and candied fruit.
3. Drop spoonfuls onto a lined baking sheet, flattening them slightly. Bake for 10-12 minutes until golden.
4. Let cool and dip half of each Florentine in melted dark chocolate. Allow to set before serving.

Quatre-Quarts (Pound Cake)

Ingredients:

- 250g unsalted butter (softened)
- 250g granulated sugar
- 250g all-purpose flour
- 4 large eggs
- 1 tsp baking powder
- Zest of 1 lemon (optional)

Instructions:

1. Preheat the oven to 180°C (350°F). In a bowl, cream together butter and sugar until light and fluffy.
2. Add eggs one at a time, mixing well after each addition. Fold in flour, baking powder, and lemon zest if using.
3. Pour the batter into a greased loaf pan and bake for 50-60 minutes until golden and a toothpick comes out clean. Let cool before slicing.

Sablés

Ingredients:

- 250g unsalted butter (softened)
- 200g granulated sugar
- 1 large egg yolk
- 500g all-purpose flour
- 1 tsp vanilla extract
- Pinch of salt

Instructions:

1. In a bowl, cream together butter and sugar until fluffy. Add egg yolk, vanilla extract, and salt, mixing until combined.
2. Gradually add flour, mixing until a dough forms. Shape into logs, wrap in plastic, and chill for at least 30 minutes.
3. Preheat the oven to 180°C (350°F). Slice chilled dough into rounds and place on a lined baking sheet. Bake for 12-15 minutes until lightly golden. Let cool before serving.

Feuilletés

Ingredients:

- 250g puff pastry (store-bought or homemade)
- 100g cheese (Gruyère or similar)
- 1 egg (for egg wash)

Instructions:

1. Preheat the oven to 200°C (390°F). Roll out puff pastry and cut into squares or rectangles.
2. Place a small amount of cheese in the center of each piece. Fold over to form triangles or rectangles and seal the edges.
3. Brush with beaten egg for a golden finish. Bake for 15-20 minutes until puffed and golden brown. Serve warm.

www.ingramcontent.com/pod-product-compliance
Lightning Source LLC
LaVergne TN
LVHW081325060526
838201LV00055B/2464